# Channel Islands Occupied

Unique pictures of the Nazi rule 1940–1945

Compiled, and with a commentary, by Richard Mayne

# Les Iles Anglo-Normandes Occupées

Des photographies uniques du règne Nazi 1940–1945

Compilé et avec un commentaire de Richard Mayne

Jarrold and Sons Limited, Norwich

# Introduction

In 1940 Hitler's legions swept rapidly and violently through France, and on 12 June the swastika, that hated symbol of Nazi Germany, was flown from public buildings in Paris. With the fall of the rest of France imminent, the German occupation of the Channel Islands also became inevitable.

There was voluntary evacuation to Britain of the civilian population of the islands and about 34,500 people departed, leaving a population of some 64,000. In Alderney the evacuation was so thorough that only 7 people remained out of a population of 1,432. At the same time the British Government demilitarised the islands by withdrawing British troops. The Jersey Militia subsequently became the 11th Battalion of the Hampshire Regiment. The Guernsey Militia had previously been disbanded to release hundreds of men to volunteer for H.M. forces.

En 1940, les armées d'Hitler s'avancèrent rapidement à travers la France et le 12 juin, la croix gammée, symbole odieux de l'Allemagne Nazie, flottait sur Paris. Avec la chute imminente du reste de la France, l'occupation allemande des Iles Anglo-Normandes devenait inévitable. Une partie de la population civile fut évacuée en Grande-Bretagne (env. 34.500 personnes) en laissant près de 64.000 derrière eux. Les îles furent aussi démilitarisées par le retrait des troupes britanniques.

Right: *The goose-step in the Channel Islands.*

A droite: *Des soldats défilant au pas de l'oie.*

# The calm before the storm

Life on the islands continued quite normally for the first few months of the war, for the fighting was a long way off, and it was assumed that the Germans would never cross the Maginot Line. It was also believed that, even in the unlikely event of France being occupied, the Channel Islands could be of no possible use to Hitler. The islands carried on exporting their tomatoes and potatoes, and until a week before the Occupation advertised in the Press for British residents to come and spend a peaceful war away from it all.

However, in the spring of 1940 there was some alarm felt at the sight of the occasional German plane over the islands and at the reputation Goering's Stukas had built up in Europe, and it was decided to construct a few air-raid shelters and organise local A.R.P. (air-raid precautions) units.

Petrol was rationed, windows were taped over to prevent flying glass, gas-masks issued, blackout regulations put into effect and the edges of the pavements were painted white.

Right: *One of the island's air-raid shelters.*
Below: *Jersey volunteers of the A.R.P. (air-raid precautions) unit in 1940.*

A droite: *La vie continua son cours presque normalement pendant les premiers mois de guerre. Cependant, à la suite de l'apparition d'avions allemands au-dessus des îles, des abris furent construits (voir ci-contre).*
Ci-dessous: *Volontaires appartenant à une unité de défense passive à Jersey, en 1940.*

Jersey's first gas propelled car made its appearance last month
It was introduced by the Gas Company who converted one o
their own light vans with the above result.   About thirty mile
can be covered at one filling of the gas-bag.

*First signs of wartime economy – the Gas Company's first gas-propelled van.*

*Premiers signes des restrictions – la première camionnette à gaz, d'une autonomie de près de 45 km.*

The windows of the islands' shops were taped to prevent flying glass.

*On recouvrait les vitrines de papier collant pour les empêcher de voler en éclats.*

Springfield Sports Ground, Jersey, as a first-aid post and air-raid shelter.

*Le stade de Springfield à Jersey fut transformé en poste de secours et abri anti-aérien.*

# Luftwaffe over Jersey and Guernsey

Late in the afternoon of 28 June 1940 six Heinkel bombers attacked Jersey's La Rocque and the St Helier Harbour weighbridge area with bombs and machine-guns, killing ten people and injuring many more. Guernsey, attacked at the same time, suffered even greater casualties for twenty-nine people were killed. The lifeboat was also attacked on its way from Guernsey to Jersey and a member of the crew was killed.

Post-war German records suggest that the Germans were unaware that the islands were undefended at this period. German aerial observation had shown columns of transport leading to the docks; in fact, these were only potatoes and tomatoes for shipment. It is also not widely known that the first R.A.F. bombing raids on Milan and Turin had set out from Jersey and Guernsey. This occurrence possibly supported the Germans' notion that the islands were defended.

Extreme upper right: *A Dornier 17 on observation over the islands prior to the attack.*
Upper right: *St Helier during the air raid.*
Right: *Bomb damage to St Helier Harbour.*

En haut à droite: *Un Dornier 17 en observation au-dessus des îles. Les Allemands pensaient probablement à ce moment-là que les îles étaient protégées.*
Ci-dessus à droite: *Le 28 juin 1940, six bombardiers Heinkel attaquèrent Jersey en plusieurs endroits. Sur cette photographie on peut voir St Hélier pendant le raid aérien.*
A droite: *Dommages occasionnés par les bombes au port de St Hélier.*

Left: *Bomb damage at the St Helier Harbour weighbridge area*

A gauche: *Le quartier du pont-bascule endommagé par les bombes.*

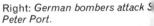

Right: *German bombers attack S Peter Port.*

A droite: *Les bombardiers allemands attaquent St Peter Po*

Right: *German bombers machin gunned this hotel in St Helier's Mulcaster Street.*

A droite: *Cet hôtel de St Hélier (situé dans Mulcaster Street) mitraillé par les bombardiers allemands.*

Left: *Bomb damage to the Clock Tower, St Peter Port, Guernsey.*

A gauche: *La Tour de l'Horloge de St Peter Port (Guernesey) endommagée par les bombes.*

Translation of a Communication addressed to th[e]
Governor of the Isle of Jersey.

1st July, 1940.

To the Chief of the Military and Civ[il]
Authorities

Jersey (St. Helier).

1. I intend to neutralize military establishments in Jersey [by]
   occupation.

2. As evidence that the Island will surrender the military a[nd]
   other establishments without resistance and without destroyi[ng]
   them, a large White Cross is to be shown as follows, from 7 a[.m.]
   July 2nd, 1940.

   a. In the centre of the Airport n the East of the Island.
   b. On the highest point of the fortifications of the port.
   c. On the square to the North of the Inner Basin of the Harbour.

   Moreover all fortifications, buildings, establishments and houses are to show the White [Cross]

3. If these signs of peaceful surrender are not observed [by]
   7 a.m. July 2nd, heavy bombardment will take place.

   a. Against all military objects.
   b. Against all establishments and objects useful for defence.

4. The signs of surrender must remain up to the time of
   occupation of the Island by German troops.

5. Representatives of the Authorities must stay at the Air[port]
   until the occupation.

6. All Radio traffic and other communications with Authori[ties]
   outside the Island will be considered hostile actions and [will]
   be followed by bombardment.

7. Every hostile action against my representatives will [be]
   followed by bombardment.

8. In case of peaceful surrender, the lives, property, and lib[erty]
   of peaceful inhabitants are solemnly guaranteed.

The Commander of the German Air Forces in Normandie,

Gene[ral]

The States have ordered this Communication to be printed and posted forthwith, and char[ge]
Inhabitants to keep calm, to comply with the requirements of the Communication and to offer n[o]
[resist]ance whatsoever to the occupation of the Island.

*A German proclamation – the first of many.*

*Une proclamation allemande – la première d'une longue suite.*

# The arrival of the Wehrmacht

On 1 July 1940 a German aircraft flew over Jersey very early in the morning and dropped three copies of a surrender ultimatum at various parts of the island. These documents were taken to the Bailiff (chief of the island's administration) who, under the threat of heavy bombardment, had no alternative but to comply with the instructions that were given. The orders were signed by the Commander of the Luftwaffe in Normandy, General von Richthofen (cousin of the famous German air ace of the First World War).

Later that same day the pilot of a Dornier from the squadron that had been observing the islands saw the white flag and crosses, which were part of the surrender terms, and the Airport looking very peaceful, and decided to land and investigate. The navigator, Oberleutnant Kern, must have been filled with apprehension as he walked from the bomber to the Airport building, his pistol at the ready.

Kern was told that the island was ready to comply with the terms of surrender, and his pilot took off to report to his superiors, subsequently returning with four Dorniers under the command of Staffelkapitän Obernitz who remained in charge at the Airport for some time.

Still later that day Junker 52 transport planes filled with soldiers arrived under the command of Hauptmann Gussek, who was Jersey's first German Kommandant. Guernsey had been occupied in a similar manner the previous evening, and Major-Doktor Lanz became the first Kommandant. The Luftwaffe landed at Alderney Airport on 2 July and Sark's occupation by sea followed on 3 July.

Right: *The arrival of the Germans at Guernsey Airport.*

*A droite: Arrivée des Allemands à l'aéroport de Guernesey.*

*White crosses had to be painted in conspicuous places under the German terms of surrender. This one is in the weighbridge area of St Helier's Harbour.*

*Pour se conformer aux exigences allemandes, il fallut peindre des croix blanches telles que celle-ci au port de St Hélier.*

*One of the first aircraft and crew to land at Jersey. The dog was the squadron mascot.*

*Un des premiers avions militaires à atterir à Jersey.*

Above: *The arrival on 1 July 1940 at Jersey Airport of the first occupying troops (Luftwaffe)*. Below left: *One of the first German pilots at the Airport*. Below right: *Guernsey's Kommandant, Major-Doktor Lanz, and his aides were the first Germans to land at Sark.*

Ci-dessus: *Le 1er juillet 1940, les premières troupes occupantes (de la Luftwaffe) arrivent à l'aéroport de Jersey*. Ci-dessous à gauche: *Un pilote allemand à l'aéroport*. Ci-dessous à droite: *Le Kommandant de Guernesey, Major-Doktor Lanz et ses aides de camp.*

*Types of German aircraft seen at Jersey Airport* – top of page, *Dornier 17;* centre, *Messerschmitt 110;* above, *Junkers 88.*

*Types d'avions allemands à l'aéroport de Jersey* – en haut: *Dornier 17;* au centre: *Messerschmitt 110;* ci-dessus: *Junkers 88.*

Above: *The Town Hall was the first German H.Q. in Jersey.* Below left: *Press Censorship. A. G. Harrison of the* Jersey Evening Post *in discussion with the Editor and Censor of the German* Inselzeitung. *Below right: The Kommandant's Headquarters at Guernsey in July 1940.*

Ci-dessus: *La mairie de Jersey, premier Quartier Général allemand.* Ci-dessous à gauche: *La censure de la presse. A. G. Harrison du* Jersey Evening Post *discute avec le rédacteur en chef de* l'Inselzeitung *allemand.* Ci-dessous à droite: *Le Quartier Général du Kommandant à Guernesey.*

# Early days

Communications were severed between the islands and England, and swastikas were flown at the airports and from public buildings. Proclamations and orders were issued for the civilian populations and soon anti-aircraft guns began to arrive, and were placed round the airports and harbours.

The first German troops were in high spirits and friendly towards the civilians for, as they frequently remarked, the occupation of Britain was but a few days away. Sites were chosen throughout the islands for pasting the orders and proclamations. These were not always of the highest standard of English; one notice threatened saboteurs with 'fusilation'. The Germans quickly organised themselves, digging trenches and requisitioning hotels and houses as billets, and after the war it was estimated that in Jersey alone 2,700 buildings had been occupied. The Reichsmark was introduced, and the eventual exchange rate was established at 1 Reichsmark to 2s. 1½d. (10½p). The onslaught that the troops made on the shops throughout the islands was so great that orders were issued limiting sales.

July 1940 saw the appearance in Jersey of the first German newspaper for the troops, printed at first on the front page of the *Jersey Evening Post*, but eventually issued as a separate news-sheet called the *Insel Zeitung*. A similar newspaper later appeared in Guernsey. All outside news was supplied by the Germans for the local newspapers and very strict censorship was maintained on all items including advertisements. One edition of about 10,000 copies of the *Jersey Evening Post* was scrapped because the German Censor objected to the wording of an advertisement he had noticed only when the whole issue had been printed.

*Marais Square, Alderney.*
*Marais Square à Alderney.*

*German sign in Jersey, proclaiming the Headquarters of the 'British' Channel Islands.*

*Signe allemand à Jersey indiquant le Quartier Général des Iles Anglo-Normandes « Britanniques ».*

Right: Langsam fahren – *Drive slowly. Traffic sign repeated in German, for the benefit of military drivers, painted on the road in St Helier.*

A droite: *Vitesse réduite – signes au sol à St Hélier, répétés en allemand.*

## BEKANNTMACHUNG:

Der Angeklagte
LOUIS BERRIER
wohnhaft in Ernes
hat eine Brieftaube mit
Nachrichten für England
fliegen lassen.

Er wurde vom Kriegs-
gericht deshalb wegen
Spionage

## ZUM TODE

verurteilt und am
2. August 1941
erschossen.

den 3 August 1941    Das Kriegsgericht

## NOTICE:

LOUIS BERRIER,
a resident of Ernes
is charged with having
released a pigeon with
a message for England.
He was, therefore, sentenced

## TO DEATH

for espionage by the
Court Martial and

## SHOT

on the 2nd of August.

August 3rd 1941    Court M...

---

More of the hated proclamations and death warnings, which were to be seen on the islands.
Below: *François Scornet was eventually executed in the grounds of Jersey's St Ouen's Manor.*
Right: *St Peter Port echoing to the jackboot in July 1940.*

*Proclamations et menaces de mort allemandes émises dans les îles.*
Ci-dessous: *Avis informant que le Français François Scornet a été exécuté par les Allemands pour son soutien à l'Angleterre.*
A droite: *Des Allemands à St Peter Port, juillet 1940.*

---

Orders of the Comm... ...nt of
the German Forces in ...cupation
of the Island of Jersey.

1. All Inhabitants must be indoors by 11 p.m. and must not leave their homes before 5 a.m.
2. We will respect the population in Jers... ...attempt to cause the least trouble, se... taken.
3. All orders given by the Military Auth... obeyed.
4. All spirits must be locked up immediatel... supplied, obtained or consumed hencef... does not apply to stocks in private house...
5. No person shall enter the Aerodrome a...
6. All Rifles, Airguns, Revolvers, Dagger... other Weapons whatsoever, except So... with all Ammunition, be delivered at ... 12 Noon to-morrow, July 3rd.
7. All British S...ors, Airmen and Soldie... Officers, in ...'s Island must report ... Office, Tow... ...ll, at 10 a.m. to-morrow.
8. No Boat or ...ssel of any description, ... Boat, shall ...ve The Harbours or any ... same is moo... ...ithout an Order from ... to be obtain... ...Commandant, ... ...must rem... Boats arri... ...leave. The crew ...to the Harbo...

The Sale of Motor Spirit ... ...ified, except for ... the Delivery of Food ...
the Military Author...

The use o... ...ivate...

The Black-out Re, ... ...dly in force ...
Banks and Shops ... ...as before...
In order to confor... ...al European Time ...
Hour at 11 p.m. T... ...
It is Forbidden to Li ... ...less Transmitting Stations.
Stations.

The Raising of Prices ... ...lities is Fo...

(Signed)
THE GERM... COMMAND ...T...

1st July, 1940.

To the Chief of the Military and Civi...

...r).

Jersey b...

...litary an...
...destroyin...
...from 7 a.m...

the White Fla...
...served by...
...ce.

...me of th...

...he Airpor...

Authoritie...
...s and wil...

...sentatives will ...

...roperty, and 'liberty...
...antee'd...

...andie,
...General

## BEKANNTMACHUNG:

FRANÇOIS SCORNET,
geb. 25-5-1919, zuletzt wohnhaft in
Ploujean (Departement Finistere) ist
wegen Begunstigung des Feindes durch
beabsichtigte Unterstutzung Englands
im Kriege gegen das Deutsche Reich
durch das Kriegsgericht

## ZUM TODE

verurteilt und am 17-III-1941
erschossen worden.

Das Kriegsgericht.

Den 23-III-1941.

## PUBLICATION:

The population is herewith notified, that
FRANÇOIS SCORNET,
born on May 25th 1919, residing in
Ploujean (Department Finistere) has
been sentenced

## TO DEATH

by the German War Court and has
been shot on March 17th, 1941. This
had to be done, because of his favouring
the actions of the enemy by wilfully
supporting England in the war against
the German Empire.

German War Court.

March 23rd, 1941.

7. Every host... ...ction ...
...ollowed b... ...abardmer ...
...case of ...eful surr...
peaceful ...habitants ar...
The Commande...

The States have ordered this Communication to be printed and posted ...
Inhabitants  to  ...

Above: *Queueing for skimmed milk.*
Below: *Guernsey in 1940.*

Ci-dessus: *On fait la queue pour du lait écrémé, à Jersey en 1941.* Ci-dessous: *Guernesey en 1940.*

Above: *First of the anti-Jewish measures.* Below: *A Jersey cinema decorated to celebrate the Führer's birthday.*

Ci-dessus: *« Commerce juif » – tous les magasins appartenant à des juifs étaient obligés de l'annoncer.* Ci-dessous: *Un des cinémas de Jersey décoré pour l'anniversaire du Führer.*

*The Dame of Sark with German officers at La Seigneurie.*

*La Dame de Sercq en compagnie d'officiers allemands à La Seigneurie.*

*Fl. Oberhauser*

FELDKOMMANDANTUR 515.
NEBENSTELLE GUERNSEY.

N° 1476

# TABAKWAREN—BEZUGSCHEIN.
## TOBACCO PERMITS.

für Wehrmachtsangehörige auf der Insel Guernsey.
for members of the German Forces on the Island of Guernsey

Gültig für Monat Januar 1941.
for the Month of January 1941.

Tagesrationssätz : 20 Zigaretten oder : 20 Cigarettes or
Daily Rations : 5 Zigarren oder : 5 Cigars or
10 Zigarillos oder : 10 Cigarillos or
1 Oz. Tabak : 1 oz. Tobacco.

Es dürfen nicht mehr als 5 Tagesrationssätze auf
einmal beliefert werden.
It is not permitted to sell more than 5 daily rations
at one time.

Feldpostdienststempel der Einheit.
Field Post Stamp, Unit.

Above: *German soldier's Tobacco Ration card, January 1941.*
Above right: *German Driving Permit to be attached to the windscreen.*
Right: *Wartime Identity Card belonging to Mrs Le Tessier, of Guernsey.*
Below: *Anti-aircraft guns stored in a German tunnel in Jersey.*

Ci-dessus: *Carte de tabac d'un soldat allemand.*
Ci-dessus à droite: *Permis de conduire allemand à afficher au pare-brise.*
A droite: *Carte d'identité de guerre appartenant à Madame Le Tessier de Guernesey.*
Ci-dessous: *Canon des contre-avions allemand.*

# FAHRERLAUBNIS
## DRIVING PERMIT

List No. 26.

The Austin

No. 1540. has a

Permit for further use up to **31st OCTOBER, 1940**

ld Kommandantur 515
Nebenstelle Guernsey.

States Controller
Petroleum Supplies

Banks, Brownsey & Co. Ltd., Printers, Guernsey.

---

No. 17360

The holder of this Card is
Inhaber dieser Karte ist    LE TISSIER. ETHEL. MAY.    D

Residing at
Wohnhaft    Herston. Vâtel.

Born on the
Geboren am    8. 4. 1890    at
in    Radstock. Somerset.

### PARTICULARS—NÄHERE ANGA

M....Single, Married, Widow or Widower

....Ledig, verheiratet, verwitwet

Dark Brown....Colour of Hair

Dunkelbraun....Farbe des Haares

Grey....Colour of Eyes

Grau....Farbe der Augen

E. M. Le Tissier

Controlling Committee of
the States of Guernsey.

Feldkommandantur,
Nebenstelle Guernsey.

# German Command

*Military Commanders of the Channel Islands*
The following German officers were in command of the Channel Islands during the Occupation:
Colonel Graf von Schmettow; from 27 September 1940 until 1 July 1941.
Major-General Erich Müller; from 1 July 1941 until 4 September 1943.
Major-General Graf von Schmettow; from 4 September 1943 to 28 February 1945.
Vice-Admiral Hüffmeier; from 28 February 1945 until the Liberation in May 1945.

The 9 August 1940 saw the establishment in Jersey of Feldkommandantur 515, whose task was the detailed administration of the Channel Islands. The staff consisted of selected German officers, most having held administrative, legal and advisory posts in civilian life, and the first Kommandant was Colonel (later Major-General) Schumacher who resigned on 4 October 1941. His successor was Colonel (later Major-General) Knackfüss who remained until the Feldkommand was reduced to a Platzkommand in 1944, when Captain (later Major) Heider took charge. Major Heider was replaced on 28 February 1944 by Korvetten-Kapitän von Kleve who remained Platzkommandant until the Liberation.

Les officiers allemands suivants furent à la tête des Iles Anglo-Normandes pendant l'occupation:
Le Colonel Graf von Schmettow; du 27 septembre 1940 au 1 juillet 1941.
Le Général Erich Müller; du 1 juillet 1941 au 4 septembre 1943.
Le Général Graf von Schmettow; du 4 septembre 1943 au 28 février 1945.
Le Vice-Amiral Hüffmeier; du 28 février 1945 à la libération.

Le 9 août 1940, le Feldkommandantur 515 s'établit à Jersey, avec pour tâche l'administration des Iles Anglo-Normandes. Le personnel se composait d'officiers sélec-tionnés, avec le Colonel Schumacher, puis le Colonel Knackfüss à sa tête. Le Feldkommand fut réduit au grade de Platzkommand en 1944.

*Dr Fritz Todt supervising emplacement of 2 ex-French '75' field guns at South Hill, Jersey in 1941.*

*Le docteur Fritz Todt, passant les canons er revue à South Hill, Jersey, 1941.*

*Major-General Müller, who was later sent to Russia.*

*Le Général de Division Müller, envoyé par la suite en Russie.*

...illor Pelz, Chief Agricultural Officer, with
...rführer Hertzog in Alderney.

...seiller Pelz, officier en charge de l'agriculture,
...rney.

Colonel Ziegler, seen mounted, reviewing troops
in St Helier in 1940.

Le Colonel Ziegler passant les troupes en revue à
St Hélier en 1940.

...siting General Stülpnagel, Commander of
...rn France, who was later executed for his part
...lot on Hitler's life.

...éral Stülpnagel, Commandant du Nord de la
... en visite.

Colonel Knackfüss at the Officers Club,
Bagatelle. He was killed in Russia in 1944.

Le Colonel Knackfüss au Club des Officiers à
Bagatelle. Il fut tué en Russie en 1944.

# Fortifications

Under a direct order from Hitler the islands were to be turned into an impregnable fortress to be completed in eight years. As with the building of the Atlantic Wall the job was entrusted to the Organisation Todt, directed by Dr Fritz Todt, the highly successful engineer who had built the Autobahns. The British have no equivalent of the Organisation Todt, which comprised architects, builders and allied tradesmen of every description. The greater part of this work, that is the actual manual labour, was delegated after 1940 to what could only be described as 'slave labour' in these islands, consisting mainly of Russians, Frenchmen and Spanish Republicans. These workers were treated extremely cruelly and as subhuman by all branches of the German forces. German records state that in 1942 there were 3,270 foreign workers in Jersey alone, and millions of tons of materials poured into these islands from France. Various Lagers or compounds sprang up all over the islands to house workers and equipment.

As well as the 'slave' camps a concentration camp named 'SYLT' was established in Alderney for 500 political prisoners (not Islanders), and these too were engaged upon the construction of fortifications. The camp was staffed by the S.S. and was a branch of the notorious Neuengamme Concentration Camp in Germany. It was disbanded in July 1944.

Above right: *A bunker at Jersey's Gorey Pier – notice the painted windows.*
Right: *Germans repairing La Coupée, Sark.*
Extreme right: *Colonel Knackfüss watches the progress of fortifications in 1942.*

Ci-dessus à droite: *Blockhaus à la jetée Gorey à Jersey.*
A droite: *Des Allemands en train de réparer La Coupée, à Sercq.*
Extrême-droite: *Hitler ordonna que les îles fussent transformées en forteresses imprenables; on voit ici la construction de fortifications.*

Danger, Mines – 50,000 were laid in Jersey.

Danger, Mines – on en posa 50.000 à Jersey.

A rare photograph of the graves of some of Alderney's 'slave' workers.

Une photographie rare des tombes de quelques-uns des travailleurs « esclaves » d'Alderney.

German superimposed plan of ammunition tunnels built by 'slave' workers under St Saviour's Church, Guernsey.

Plan allemand des tunnels de munitions à Guernesey, sous l'église.

*The Organisation Todt, which was in charge of the building of fortifications.*

*L'Organisation Todt, responsable de la construction de fortifications.*

*Funeral of a German member of the Organisation Todt at Jersey's St Brelade's Cemetery.*

*Enterrement d'un des membres allemands de l'Organisation Todt, au cimetière St Brelade à Jersey.*

# The weapons of war

A complete German infantry division was stationed on the Channel Islands throughout the war. This was the 319th Infantry (later Grenadier) Division, of about 21,000 men of the Seventh Army, supported by tank troops, artillerymen, naval coastal artillerymen, anti-aircraft gunners, signal troops, Luftwaffe and naval personnel.

The islands were the most heavily fortified area in western Europe and if one looks at a map of western France the reason becomes evident. The sweep of the German heavy guns, especially the Mirus battery in Guernsey, could protect the area extending from Cherbourg in Normandy round the coast to Cap Frehel in Brittany, thereby dispensing with the protection of hundreds of miles of coastline.

The following enumeration of artillery illustrates the strength of Jersey's defence: fifteen batteries of heavy artillery totalling fifty-nine guns comprising four 22 cm K532(f) ex-French guns at La Moye (these were the largest calibre in Jersey); nine 21 cm Morser-18 German guns (three at St Martin, three near Red Houses and three near St Ouen's Church); four 15·5 cm K418(f) ex-French guns at Les Landes; eight 15 cm K18 German guns (four at La Coupe and four near Verclut); four 15 cm SKL45 German naval guns at Noirmont; four 10·5 cm K331(f) ex-French guns at Westmount; twenty 10 cm 14/18(t) Czechoslovakian guns in five batteries (four near Maufant, four at Teighmore, four near Blanchpierre, four near La Pulente and four at Grouville Arsenal); six 8 cm FK30(t) Czechoslovakian guns (four at La Haule and two at St Aubin).

These were all heavy artillery but there were also eighty anti-tank and invasion defence guns comprising thirty ex-French 10·5 cm K331(f)s, twelve German 7·5 cm Pak 40s, twelve German 5 cm Pak 38s and twenty-six Czechoslovakian 4·7 cm anti-tanks. The air defence or 'flak' consisted of eleven batteries totalling 137 guns of which thirty-six were the famous 8·8 cm used with such deadly effect in the tank battles of the 'Afrika Korps.'

Above: *An 8·8 cm anti-aircraft gun in Jersey with its Luftwaffe crew. The 'kills' ringed on barrel were obviously obtained elsewhere.*
Right: *A German 15 cm K18 at Verclut, Jersey.*

*Les Iles Anglo-Normandes furent la région plus fortifiée d'Europe Occidentale. Voici certaines armes utilisées alors. Ci-dessus: Canon D.C.A. de 8,8 cm avec son unité du Luftwaffe.*
*A droite: K18 allemand de 15 cm à Verclut (Jersey).*

Light 'flak' gun at Castle Cornet, Guernsey.

Canon D.C.A. à Castle Cornet (Guernesey).

Above: *48 ton, 12 inch gun of Mirus Battery, Guernsey. Photograph taken clandestinely by Mr Frank le Page, a St Martin's grocer.*
Below: *German radar 'Wurtzburg' in Jersey.*

Ci-dessus: *Canon long de 30 cm pesant 48 tonnes, de la Batterie de Mirus, Guernesey. Photographie prise clandestinement par M. Frank le Page, épicier de St Martin.*
Ci-dessous: *Radar allemand (« Wurtzburg ») à Jersey.*

Large German gun near Telegraph Bay, Alderney.

*Gros canon allemand.*

A 3·7 cm anti-tank gun at La Seigneurie, Sark.

*Canon anti-chars de 3,7 cm.*

Ex-French 'Char B' tanks, with a 7·5 cm howitzer in the hull and a 4·7 cm gun in the turret. They each had a crew of four and weighed 34 tons.

*Ancien Chars B français, avec un obusier de 7,5 cm dans la coque et un canon de 4,7 cm dans la tourelle.*

Above: *A 4·7 cm self-propelled gun on a Renault 35 tank chassis. It had a crew of three or four and weighed 10 tons. There were nine in Jersey. Below: An R.A.F. Beaufort raid on ships at St Peter Port Harbour, Guernsey, in January 1942 – note stick bombs leaving aircraft.*

Ci-dessus: *Canon autonome de 4,7 cm sur châssis de tank Renault 35 (il y en avait 9 à Jersey). Ci-dessous: Raid de la R.A.F. sur des navires dans le port de St Peter Port (Guernesey) en janvier 1942.*

*Members of the Feldkommand, Alderney.*

*Membres de la Feldkommand à Alderney.*

*St Peter's Hotel, Jersey, where the Bunker War Museum is now situated – note anti-aircraft machine-gun on the roof.*

*L'hôtel St Peter à Jersey, avec un canon D.C.A. sur le toit.*

*St Peter Port, Guernsey, under new management.*

*St Peter Port, Guernesey, sous une nouvelle administration.*

# Requisitioned buildings

Most of the hotels in the islands were taken over by the German forces. The majority were used as billets while others became Soldatenheims (of which the British equivalent would be the N.A.A.F.I.), hospitals, regimental headquarters and supply depots. One was used by the Organisation Todt and some even became brothels staffed by imported foreign girls. Many hotels had exclusive underground systems constructed, and one hotel was later demolished to make way for the German railway.

La plupart des hôtels des îles furent réquisitionnés par les Allemands pour servir de logements, hôpitaux, dépôts, quartiers généraux, etc. L'un d'eux fut utilisé par l'Organisation Todt et certains devinrent même des maisons closes.

Above right: *Delousing station in St Helier for foreign workers.*
Right: *Montague Burton's as a German bookshop.*
Extreme right: *Pomme d'Or Hotel, the German Naval H.Q. in Jersey.*

Ci-dessus à droite: *Centre d'épouillage pour travailleurs étrangers à St Hélier.*
A droite: *Le magasin de Montague Burton transformé en librairie allemande.*
Extrême droite: *L'hôtel Pomme d'Or, quartier général de la marine allemande à Jersey.*

# German railways

*The German railway bridge across St Helier Harbour.*

*Pont ferroviaire allemand au port de St Hélier.*

*A locomotive decorated for the opening of the German railway in Jersey on 15 July 1942.*

*Locomotive décorée pour l'ouverture du chemin de fer allemand à Jersey en 1942.*

Railways were built in Jersey and Guernsey by the Todt Organisation. Jersey had a metre-gauge line which went from St Helier to Ronez Quarry with branches to Corbière and Tesson Mill. Another was a 60 cm gauge line which went to the Western Quarries from La Pulente along St Ouen's Bay and a third was a 60 cm gauge line which ran eastward from St Helier to Gorey.

In Guernsey the main lines were of 90 cm gauge and the less important lines were of 60 cm. In both islands the railways were built initially to transport the vast amount of materials necessary for the construction of the hundreds of concrete fortifications, which still scar these islands.

On 15 July 1942 the St Helier to Millbrook line was officially inaugurated by the Military Commander, Colonel Graf von Schmettow, accompanied by a host of officials of the three services, plus the representatives of the Todt Organisation. The German report in the local newspaper extolled this brilliant German idea, which would bring such great benefits to the island, little knowing that the island's railways had been scrapped with the advent of motor buses years before.

The Abergeldie Hotel at the Dicq was demolished to make way for the line, and a tunnel was bored under Mount Bingham. A favourite game of local children was to place coins and sometimes stones on the rails, which caused many derailments.

Locomotives for the metre gauge were all French, and the 60 cm gauge locomotives were Deutz diesels. The rolling stock consisted mainly of open trucks of French origin, and the word 'Posen' was painted in large letters on their sides.

L'Organisation Todt construisit le réseau de chemins de fer de Jersey et Guernesey pour transporter les matériaux nécessaires à la construction des fortifications.

*Jersey 1945:* (above) *German (ex-French) engine;* (below) *German prisoners removing track.*

*Jersey, 1945:* (ci-dessus) *Locomotive allemande (ex-française);* (ci-dessous) *prisonniers allemands en train d'enlever une voie.*

# Deportations

Undoubtedly the greatest shock, inducing the lowest morale in the population, came with a German order published in the island newspapers of 15 September 1942. It stated 'All those men not born on the Channel Islands, from 16 to 70 years of age who belong to the English people, and their families, will be evacuated and transferred to Germany.'

The next morning soldiers and local police started serving evacuation notices telling people to present themselves, some of them the same day, with their ration books, only the luggage they could carry and a limit of fifty Reichsmarks. A great panic ensued and much distress was caused by this sudden and ruthless action.

Local officials protested, but to no avail, as this was a direct order from Hitler's Headquarters. Apparently this was a reprisal for the imprisonment of Germans in Persia (Iran).

Feeling ran so high against the order that for the first time there were public demonstrations, and arrests were made. From Jersey a total of 1,186 persons were deported to three internment camps in Germany. The single men were sent to Laufen, and families and single women to Wurzach and Biberach. Fortunately, they were supported by Red Cross food parcels and except for their lack of freedom did not fare too badly. They were even able on occasions to send food and cigarettes from their camps back to the islands.

Right: *Scenes at the Terminus Building, St Helier, during the deportations of British-born residents to Germany in September 1942. Most of the Channel Island deportees were sent to one of three internment camps.*

A droite: *Le Terminus à St Hélier, après qu'on ait ordonné en septembre 1942, que tous les résidents de nationalité britannique soient déportés en Allemagne. Les déportés étaient envoyés dans l'un des trois camps d'internement qui leur étaient spécialement destinés.*

Above: *Channel Island internees at work in Biberach Camp in 1945.*
Below: *French liberators at the north wing of Wurzach Castle.*

Ci-dessus: *Prisonniers des Iles Anglo-Normandes au travail, au camp de Biberach en 1945.*
Ci-dessous: *Libérateurs français dans l'aile Nord du château de Wurzach.*

Above: *Internees of Wurzach Camp about to leave for England after being liberated by French tanks on 28 April 1945.*
Below: *French Army trucks conveying Channel Islanders from Wurzach Camp.*

Ci-dessus: *Prisonniers du camp de Wurzach après leur libération par des chars français le 28 avril 1945.*
Ci-dessous: *Anciens prisonniers des îles, transportés par des camions de l'armée française du camp de Wurzach avant d'être rapatriés par avion en Grande-Bretagne.*

# The sound of the Jackboot

The garrison of the islands consisted mainly of units of the German Army, with some Luftwaffe personnel whose main task appeared to be anti-aircraft defence (in contrast to the British forces where the Army mans the anti-aircraft guns). A few naval personnel could also be seen around the harbour areas, and their numbers increased with the arrival of sundry units of the German Navy. Contrary to popular belief the Gestapo were not established in the islands. The characters who loved to don black rubber raincoats and black hats to induce fear into civilian and soldier alike were the Feldgendarmerie or field police. Fortunately, there were also none of the dreaded S.S. in Jersey or Guernsey but they were not too far away, for they were in charge of a concentration camp in Alderney. The early part of the war saw units of the Reichsarbeitsdienst or R.A.D. stationed in Jersey. The R.A.D. was the intermediary stage from the Hitler Youth to the Army.

Tank personnel were present to man the many ex-French tanks brought to the islands. A unit of Russians, volunteers in the German Army, could also be seen. They wore normal German uniform but with a cloth shield on their arm with the Russian letters P.O.A., meaning Russian Volunteer Army but known locally as 'Pals of Adolf'.

As Hitler lost his ships so the naval representation in the island grew, until eventually the Army Commander was replaced by a Vice-Admiral. This man's Nazi zeal and loyalty to Hitler at the period just before the Liberation came close to causing a mutiny among the German soldiery.

Above: *German Army band in Alderney.*

Ci-dessus: *Orchestre de l'armée allemande à Alderney.*

Below: *North Esplanade, Guernsey.*

Ci-dessous: *L'Esplanade Nord à Guernesey.*

Above: *March past of the Luftwaffe at Jersey in 1940.*

Ci-dessus: *Défilé de la Luftwaffe à Jersey en 1940.*

ft: *The two sides of the law in Jersey – P.C. Renouf and Dr Bleckwenn of Feldkommand 515.*
ɔove: *German officers at La Coupée on Sark in 1941.*
·low: *Luftwaffe Band Concert on Royal Parade at St Helier in 1942.*

gauche: *Les deux aspects de la loi à Jersey – l'agent de police Renouf et le Dr Bleckwenn de la Feldkommand*
5.
-dessus: *Officiers allemands à La Coupée (Sercq) en 1941.*
-dessous: *Concert donné par l'orchestre de la Luftwaffe à St Hélier en 1942.*

Left: *Gateway to Alderney's concentration camp SYLT.*

A gauche: *Entrée du camp de concentration d'Alderney (SYLT*

Right: *Russian 'slave' workers with German troops in Guernse*

A droite: *Travailleurs « esclaves » russes à Guernesey*

Left: *A group of Spanish 'slave workers', from Camp UDET, at Jersey in 1942.*

A gauche: *Groupe de travailleu « esclaves » espagnols à Jersey 1942.*

Right: *German vessel seen in Herm Harbour early in 1943.*

A droite: *Navire allemand dans port d'Herm, début 1943.*

Left: *German officers at Creux Harbour, Sark.*

A gauche: *Officiers allemands port de Creux à Sercq.*

Right: *Funeral in November 19 in Jersey of Oberleutnant Zepernick who was A.D.C. to Kommandant. He was killed o train in France by the R.A.F.*

A droite: *Enterrement, à Jers en 1943, de l'Oberleutnant Zepernick, ancien aide de cam du Kommandant.*

# Invasion

The invasion of France was welcomed joyfully by the population and made even more pleasurable by the apprehension apparent on the faces of the Germans. Entertainments, games and the like were prohibited and all troops were on duty and guards were doubled. Hundreds of Allied aircraft were seen crossing over the islands, and as the days went by and the Allies were getting closer great excitement prevailed.

The concentration camp in Alderney was disbanded and many of the pitiful figures in their blue and white striped clothes were sent back to France.

Field-Marshals Rommel and von Rundstedt appealed urgently to Hitler for the 20,000 idle troops in the Channel Islands to help stem the tide of the Allied advance in Normandy, but to no avail. Hitler's anchored battleships were to remain fully staffed.

The German garrison at St Malo surrendered on 16 August 1944. Gunfire and smoke could be seen from the island and vibrations felt as Allied bombers did their work. Six hundred German wounded arrived in Jersey from St Malo and many vessels, with about 2,000 personnel, fled to Jersey for shelter and remained there.

As the battle passed on and the whole of France became cut off from these islands, an uneasy peace descended, and it must be admitted a certain disappointment, for the Islanders thought that perhaps they had been forgotten. But as is now known, great loss of life would have ensued had the Allies attempted an invasion. In Jersey alone, over 400 pieces of artillery were waiting, with 30,000 tons of ammunition and three spare barrels for each gun.

Conditions rapidly deteriorated; food-supplies could not reach the islands, and depleted stocks had to be extended still further.

L'arrivée des Alliés en France en 1944 fut accueillie avec joie par la population des Iles Anglo-Normandes.

# Bekanntmachung

(1) Um elektrischen Strom zu sparen, werden ab sofort sämtliche Theater und Lichtspielhäuser geschlossen, sowie alle Tanz- und sonstigen öffentlichen Veranstaltungen eingestellt.

(2) Die Sperrstunde wird auf 22.00 Uhr vorverlegt. Die Wirtschaften haben um 21½ Uhr zu schliessen.

Platzkommandantur I St. Helier.
7. Juni 1944.

# NOTICE

(1) With immediate effect all theatre and cinemas will close down in order to save electrical energy. All dance and other public entertainments are cancelled.

(2) Curfew hour is advanced to 10.00 p.m. Restaurants and public houses must close at 9.30 p.m.

Der Platzkommandant,

HEIDER,
Major.

German invasion panic.

*L'arrivée des Alliés affola les Allemands qui émirent soudain des ordres concernant couvre-feu, « black-out » et fermeture des lieux publics.*

Jersey, 22.6.44.

den 22. Juni 1944.

# Bekanntmachung

Betr.: Verhalten der Zivilbevölkerung auf der Strasse bei Flak-Schiessen und im Alarmfalle.

1.) Die Bevölkerung wird in ihrem eigenen Interesse vor dem Heraustreten aus den Häusern und Herumstehen auf der Strasse bei Flak-Schiessen gewarnt.
Desgleichen hat jedes Hinausschauen bei Nacht aus beleuchteten Zimmern zu unterbleiben.
Verstösse werden gemäss der Verordnung über die Verdunkelungsvorschriften bestraft werden.

2 Bei Eintritt von Kampfhandlungen und bei Ertönen von Luftschutzwarnsirenen (auf- und absteigende Töne) darf die Strasse von der Zivilbevölkerung nicht mehr betreten werden. Die Wiederfreigabe der Strasse wird durch Entwarnungssirenen (gleichbleibender Ton) bekanntgegeben.

# NOTICE

re: Danger to civilians through anti aircraft fire.

1.) In their own interest civilians are warned not to leave their houses and not to stand about in the streets when anti-aircraft guns are firing.
It is further prohibited to look out from lighted rooms at night. Infractions of this Order will be punished according to the black-out regulations.

2.) In the event of fighting and at the sounding of the air-raid sirens (fluctuating note) civilians may not go out into the streets. Permission to go out again will be given by the all-clear signal (sustained note).

Der Kommandant der Festung Jersey,
HEINE, Oberst.

# AUFRUF
## AN DIE BEVOELKERUNG DER INSEL JERSEY

---

Der Feind Deutschlands steht im Begriff, französischen Boden anzugreifen.

Ich erwarte von der Bevölkerung der Insel Jersey, dass sie unbedingt ruhig bleibt und auch bei Uebergreifen des Kampfes auf die Insel sich jeder feindlichen Haltung und Sabotage gegenüber der deutschen Wehrmacht enthält.

Bei Auftreten der geringsten Anzeichen von Unruhen werde ich die Strassen für jeden Verkehr sperren und Geiseln festnehmen lassen.

Angriffe auf die Wehrmacht werden mit dem Tode bestraft.

Der Kommandant der Festung Jersey,

Jersey, den 6. Juni 1944.

HEINE,
Oberst.

---

# PROCLAMATION
## TO THE POPULATION OF THE ISLE OF JERSEY

---

Germany's enemy is on the point of attacking French soil.

I expect the population of Jersey to keep its head, to remain calm, and to refrain from any acts of sabotage and from hostile acts against the German Forces, even should the fighting spread to Jersey.

At the first signs of unrest or trouble I will close the streets to every traffic and will secure hostages.

Attacks against the German Forces will be punished by death.

Der Kommandant der Festung Jersey,

(Signed) HEINE,
Oberst.

Jersey, 6th June, 1944.

*S.S. Vega which brought Red Cross parcels to save many Islanders' lives.*

*Le S.S. Vega sauva la vie de nombreux habitants des îles en apportant des colis de la Croix Rouge.*

*The first distribution of parcels was made in January 1945.*

*Première distribution de colis en janvier 1945.*

*In Jersey Red Cross supplies were stored in Patriotic Street.*

*Approvisionnement de Jersey par la Croix Rouge.*

# Red Cross supplies

In November 1944 the Bailiffs of the islands drafted urgent messages to the German Command for transmission to the Allies. The Jersey message read as follows:

*Sufficient anaesthetics until middle of January but only for urgent operations. Many most essential drugs now exhausted, butter stocks will be exhausted end of December, no margarine, soap exhausted except for hospitals, no gas since September, electricity will fail middle of January, no matches. Supplies of footwear and textiles practically exhausted. General state of public health causing increasing anxiety to Insular Government. Favour of a reply requested.*

Eventually agreement was reached between the British and German Governments to allow a Red Cross ship to leave Lisbon on 7 December 1944 with 750 tons of food parcels, and in December a Swedish vessel, the S.S. *Vega*, on charter to the International Red Cross, brought to the Islanders the long-awaited supplies. This occasion caused indescribable joy and relief on the part of the civilian population who had probably just spent the most miserable Christmas in the islands' history. The first issue was made in January 1945, four months before the Liberation.

Après l'arrivée des Alliés en France, les îles cessèrent de recevoir vivres et autres provisions et la situation se détériora rapidement. Finalement un accord entre les gouvernements allemand et britannique permit à un navire de la Croix Rouge de quitter Lisbone en décembre 1944 et d'apporter 750 tonnes de vivres qui furent distribuées en janvier 1945 (quatre mois avant la libération) et soulagèrent de nombreux habitants.

Above: *Transport of all types was used to fetch the long-awaited gifts.* Below: *Colonel Iselin of the International Red Cross with officials, discussing the unloading of the S.S.* Vega.

Ci-dessus: *Toutes sortes de moyens de transport furent utilisés pour la distribution des colis.* Ci-dessous: *Le Colonel Iselin de la Croix Rouge Internationale, entouré d'officiels.*

# Liberation

'Operation Nest Egg' was the name chosen for the Liberation. Task Force 135 trained for many months to carry out this task, and did not expect a vigorous defence as the operation was only to be carried out after the expected surrender of the German garrison. On 8 May 1945 the destroyer H.M.S. *Bulldog* and escort H.M.S. *Beagle* left Plymouth to rendezvous four miles off Guernsey with the Germans. Vice-Admiral Hüffmeier wanted an armistice but eventually settled the following day for a full surrender. Guernsey was liberated first by British soldiers led by Colonels Power and Stoneman. Colonel Power later phoned the Bailiff of Jersey and told him that the destroyer H.M.S. *Beagle* was on its way. The Jersey Bailiff went in a German pinnace out to the British destroyer with the Solicitor-General, the Attorney-General, the German Major-General Wolfe and two Staff officers to surrender the island.

When the first two British naval officers landed in Jersey they were mobbed by the joyful crowd. Later that afternoon Colonel W. V. A. Robinson, M.C., with the first Liberation troops, arrived.

Dame Sybil Hathaway of Sark hoisted the Union Jack and the Stars and Stripes to celebrate the Liberation, but it was not until the following day that Colonel Allen took a naval tug to Sark. The Dame spoke fluent German and was able to interpret the surrender terms. Alderney's garrison of about 3,500 Germans under Oberstleutnant Schwalm surrendered to Brigadier Snow and his tiny invasion fleet of an armed trawler and two infantry landing-craft on 16 May 1945. It was not until December that returning Islanders were able to set foot on Alderney.

The war in the Channel Islands was over.

Le 8 mai 1945, les deux navires britanniques H.M.S. *Bulldog* et H.M.S. *Beagle* quittèrent Plymouth pour rencontrer les Allemands au large de Guernesey. Ceux-ci se rendirent le lendemain. La guerre dans les Iles Anglo-Normandes était finie.

*Major-General Heine shows his papers to an Intelligence officer on board the destroyer H.M.S.* Bulldog *off Guernsey.*

*Le Général Heine montrant ses papiers à bord du H.M.S.* Bulldog.

*Charing Cross, St Helier, at 3 p.m. on 8 May 1945 – Islanders listen to loud-speakers relaying Churchill's speech:* 'and our dear Channel Islands are also to be freed today'.

*Charing Cross (St Hélier) à 15h le 8 mai 1945 – des haut-parleurs transmettent l'annonce de la libération par Churchill.*

*Jersey officials and the German Major-General Wolfe on their way to H.M.S.* Beagle *on 9 May 1945.*

*Le Général Wolfe, en compagnie d'officiels de Jersey, se rendant au navire H.M.S.* Beagle.